MT. ACONCAGUA
ARGENTINA / HEIGHT: 22,840 FEET / 6,962 METERS

MT. DENALI
(MCKINLEY) - UNITED STATES (ALASKA)
HEIGHT: 20,310 FEET / 6,190 METERS

MT. ELBRUS
RUSSIA / HEIGHT: 18,510 FEET / 5,642 METERS

MT. EVEREST
NEPAL/TIBET
HEIGHT: 29,032 FEET / 8,849 METERS

MT. KILIMANJARO
TANZANIA / HEIGHT: 19,341 FEET / 5,895 METERS

THE SEVEN SUMMITS

These mountains represent the highest peaks on each of the seven continents. Climbing all seven is a major goal for mountaineers worldwide.

MT. KOSCIUSZKO
AUSTRALIA (MAINLAND)
HEIGHT: 7,310 FEET / 2,228 METERS

MT. VINSON
ANTARCTICA / HEIGHT: 16,050 FEET / 4,892 METERS

MOUNT ACONCAGUA

THE SEVEN SUMMITS

MELISSA GISH

CREATIVE EDUCATION • CREATIVE PAPERBACKS

Published by Creative Education and Creative Paperbacks
P.O. Box 227, Mankato, Minnesota 56002
Creative Education and Creative Paperbacks
are imprints of The Creative Company
www.thecreativecompany.us

Design by Graham Morgan
Art direction by Blue Design (www.bluedes.com)

Images by Dreamstime/Extezy, 1, Pablo Sebastian Rodriguez, 19, Pecorb, cover, 1; Getty Images/Andrew Peacock, 2, Cavan Images, 38–39, Christian Kober/robertharding, 26, Johnathan Ampersand Esper, 36, Patrick Bennett, 29, Photography by Simon Bond, 35, Tuul & Bruno Morandi, 24, Walter Bibikow, 22; Unsplash/CLAUDIO MOTA, 18, constantin jamar, 10, 41, 45, Gustavo Leighton, 31, Jens Peter Olesen, 43, José Ignacio Pompé, 32, Rafael Hoyos Weht, 6; Wikimedia Commons/Albert Backer, 17, Bjørn Christian Tørrissen, 4–5, Georgibulgaro, 16, John Biggar, 30, Jorge Diaz, 14–15, Joseph James Kinsey, 38, 40, Leo Wehrli, 21, Nicolas Prieto, 9, NOIRLab/AURA/NSF, 13, Rama, 25, Tomroo, 42

Every effort has been made to contact copyright holders for material reproduced in this book. Any omissions will be rectified in subsequent printings if notice is given to the publisher.

Copyright © 2025 Creative Education, Creative Paperbacks
International copyright reserved in all countries.
No part of this book may be reproduced in any form
without written permission from the publisher.

Library of Congress Cataloging-in-Publication Data
Names: Gish, Melissa, author.
Title: Mount Aconcagua / Melissa Gish.
Description: Mankato, Minnesota : Creative Education, Creative Paperbacks, 2025. | Series: The seven summits | Includes bibliographical references and index. | Audience: Ages 10–14 | Audience: Grades 4–6 | Summary: "Mount Aconcagua is South America's tallest peak and a Seven Summits mountaineering challenge. This guide for kids age 12 and up examines the mountain's geologic and climbing history. Includes a glossary, sidebars, profiles of notable climbers, and further resources"—Provided by publisher.
Identifiers: LCCN 2024023449 (print) | LCCN 2024023450 (ebook) | ISBN 9798889892694 (library binding) | ISBN 9781682776353 (paperback) | ISBN 9798889893806 (ebook)
Subjects: LCSH: Mountaineering—Argentina—Aconcagua, Mount—Juvenile literature. | Aconcagua, Mount (Argentina)—Juvenile literature.
Classification: LCC GV199.44.A72 A2643 2025 (print) | LCC GV199.44.A72 (ebook) | DDC 796.5220982/64—dc23/eng/20240610
LC record available at https://lccn.loc.gov/2024023449
LC ebook record available at https://lccn.loc.gov/2024023450

Printed in the United States of America

Snow is the most common form of precipitation on Mount Aconcagua.

CONTENTS

Introduction 8

Chapter 1: Peaks and Valleys 11

Chapter 2: Aconcagua's Echoes 20

Chapter 3: Hidden Dangers 28

Chapter 4: Race to the Summit 37

Stories of the Summit 44

Glossary 46

Selected Bibliography 47

Websites 47

Index 48

MOUNT ACONCAGUA

INTRODUCTION

The tallest peak in the Andes Mountains boasts a masterpiece of nature's artistry: a 130-foot (40-meter) wall of ice. A man clings to the handle of a razor-sharp ice tool dug into the frozen waterfall. He drives a second tool deep into the ice and then slowly bends his knee, kicking his foot cautiously. The **crampon** attached to his boot bites into the solid surface.

The climber pulls himself upward, the movement deliberate and controlled. Ice crackles under his weight, releasing a light dusting of frozen powder that disappears into the whiteness below. The man maneuvers carefully, choosing his path with the expertise of someone who has spent a lifetime among the peaks. The rhythmic sound of his curved blades and crampons penetrating the ice resonates over the landscape, a testament to the man's determination. This is the South Face of Mount Aconcagua (ah-kon-KAH-gwah)—one of the greatest challenges among the world's **Seven Summits**.

Mount Aconcagua touches the clouds and beyond.

The Andes Mountains are tall enough to affect the region's weather patterns, blocking rain from the east.

CHAPTER 1: PEAKS AND VALLEYS

The Andes Mountains account for about 13 percent of the world's mountains and comprise the longest mountain range on any of the seven continents. They extend 5,530 miles (8,900 kilometers) along western South America, from northern Venezuela through Colombia, Ecuador, Peru, Bolivia, Chile, and into Argentina. The Andes are not as tall as the Himalayas of Asia. However, their tallest peak—Mount Aconcagua, located in Argentina—is the second-tallest of the Seven Summits, after Mount Everest. It stands 22,840 feet (6,962 m) above sea level.

Like most mountains, the Andes were formed by the movement of **tectonic plates**. More than a dozen of these plates are constantly floating and moving above the melted metal core of Earth. Like puzzle pieces, the plates fit together. Sometimes one plate slips underneath another. The top plate is pushed upward. This is how the Andes were formed—and how they continue to grow taller each year.

MOUNT ACONCAGUA

The story of the Andes began about 166 million years ago, when the South American tectonic plate broke away from the African plate. Like a bulldozer drifting westward across the sea, the South American plate scooped up ocean **sediment** in its path. After drifting for more than 140 million years, it bumped into an ocean plate called the Nazca plate. The South American plate pushed over the top of the Nazca plate, carrying its huge mounds of sediment. This plate movement, called subduction, caused heat and pressure. The Nazca plate began to melt into magma. As the pressure of this melted rock built up underground, volcanoes erupted, spewing lava that flowed and cooled over and over to form hundreds of volcanic mountains. While Mount Aconcagua originated as a volcano, it is not a volcano today.

As the volcanic mountains were forming, some of the magma remained underground and turned into massive granite structures called batholiths. At the same time, the ocean sediment that had amassed on the western edge of the South American plate formed sandstone. As the South American plate continued to rise, batholiths were pushed upward beneath a blanket of sandstone. Then, over tens of millions of years, wind and rain battered the mountains and washed away the soft sandstone, exposing the hard granite peaks. Wind erosion continued to sharpen the peaks of the Andes. Because the tectonic plates are still pushing today, the height of the Andes increases about 0.4 inch (1 centimeter) each year.

HOPPING HIGH IN THE ANDES

Living just below the snow line, the mountain viscacha is one of Mount Aconcagua's few year-round inhabitants. With long ears and strong back legs, these rodents look like rabbits but are actually members of the chinchilla family. They weigh up to 7 pounds (3.2 kilograms) and can grow to about 18 inches (46 cm) long. Their bushy tails and dense fur shield them from the cold. Expert jumpers, viscachas have fleshy pads protecting their feet as they navigate their rugged habitat, feeding on grass, moss, and **lichen**.

MOUNT ACONCAGUA

Aerial view of Mount Aconcagua

Getting the exact height of Mount Aconcagua is difficult. Ice and snow cover changes seasonally. When the mountain was first scaled in 1897, *The New York Times* reported its height to be 22,422 feet (6,834 m). In 1954, reporting on a climbing team that had to be rescued, the *Times* listed the mountain's height at 22,835 feet (6,960 m). Two years later, engineers at Buenos Aires University cut that number by 7 feet (2.1 m), while a French survey team *added* almost 10 feet (3 m). As recently as 2001, a team of scientists using global positioning system technology listed the mountain at 22,840 feet (6,962 m). This number confirmed the Argentinian government's "official" height of Mount Aconcagua's northern peak.

A ridge of about 0.6 mile (1 km) in length connects the northern peak to the mountain's southern peak, which is only about 3 feet (0.9 m) shorter. In January 1947, two German climbers named Koop and Heroid scaled

MOUNT ACONCAGUA

Aconcagua's southern peak and then hiked the ridge to the northern peak. Along the way, they found a frozen llama-like animal called a guanaco. The dry air and bitter cold had preserved the animal's body (for hundreds of years, it was later discovered). Since guanacos do not live above 13,000 feet (3,962 m), the climbers agreed that someone must have led the animal to the top of the mountain. To commemorate their find, the climbers gave the ridge connecting Aconcagua's two peaks its name: Cresta del Guanaco, or Guanaco Crest.

South America's guanacos are related to the camels of Africa and Asia.

Mount Aconcagua's steep, icy South Face

Year-round snow covers the summit of Aconcagua, and glaciers bury the slopes. The permanent snow line—the height at which snow always remains—is about 18,000 feet (5,486 m). As climbers approach this height, they encounter an otherworldly sight. Tall, thin blades of hardened snow and ice stand in vast fields on the mountainside. Some of these structures, called nieves penitentes, are only knee-high, while others are up to 13 feet (4 m) tall. Penitentes form when the heat from the sun hits the snow, and, instead of melting, the snow **evaporates** in the extremely dry, cold air. This process, called sublimation, is like seeing your breath outside on a cold day. As the invisible snow vapor rises upward, the extreme cold freezes it once again, building towers of snow and ice. Climbers must carefully **navigate** penitente fields. These structures are sharp and unstable. A falling penitente can cause serious injury.

The area from below the permanent snow line to about 15,000 feet (4,572 m) is called the alpine zone. Here the terrain is dry and barren. Loose, sharp rocks blanket the steep slopes. Boulders and jagged outcroppings dot the mountainside. Even in summer, daytime temperatures typically reach no more than 40 degrees Fahrenheit (4.4 degrees Celsius) and then fall well below freezing at night. Only the toughest low-growing plants, mosses,

CHAPTER 1: PEAKS AND VALLEYS

The valleys below Mount Aconcagua provide a breeding ground for ducks and other waterbirds.

and lichens can survive. The sub-alpine zone extends below the alpine zone to about 11,500 feet (3,505 m). Here the ground is still rocky, but more vegetation grows, stabilizing the rock. Grasses and low shrubs and plants provide food for rodents such as viscachas and Andean mice.

Continuing down the mountain, the montane zone is where the landscape opens to a vast expanse of grass, bushes, and trees. This zone extends downward to about 8,000 feet (2,438 m). Herds of guanacos graze here, ever on the lookout for mountain lions, while red foxes and birds of prey hunt hares and rodents. The unique, cushion-like yareta plant grows here, as does a grass called huecú, which means "toxic" in the Araucanian language. Grazers avoid this grass because it makes them sick. The foot of Mount Aconcagua is a set of two valleys. On the north and east is Valle de las Vacas, or Valley of Cows. On the south and west is Valle de los Horcones, or Valley of Forks. These grassy valleys support an array of wildflowers that feed hummingbirds and butterflies. Temperatures can soar to nearly 100 °F (38 °C) during the summer months (December to March).

ANDEAN CONDOR

MOUNT ACONCAGUA

CHAPTER 2: ACONCAGUA'S ECHOES

The origin of Mount Aconcagua's name is not known for sure. The Ayamara people, who have lived in the Andes for at least 800 years, call the mountain *Kon-Kawa*, meaning "snowy peak." The Mapuche people, whose **culture** may have emerged as early as 600 B.C.E., named the mountain *Aconca-Hue*, or "that which comes from the other side," referring to the mountain being on the other side of a river. The most accepted origin comes from the Quechua word *Akon-Kahuak*, which means "sentinel of stone." Quechua is a group of languages that existed during the time of the Inca Empire and is still spoken by more than five million people today.

Mount Aconcagua is the centerpiece of Argentina's Aconcagua Provincial Park. Established in 1983, the park covers an area of 162,324 acres (65,690 hectares) around its namesake mountain. The park preserves a wondrous landscape of glaciers, rivers, lakes, and rare plants and animals. Wildlife flourishes in the park, thanks to the runoff of the area's slow-melting major glaciers—Horcones Inferior and Superior, Cows, and Polish—as well as more

Vintage photo of Mount Aconcagua, 1924

CHAPTER 2: ACONCAGUA'S ECHOES

MOUNTAIN MEMORIAL

The Andinistas Cemetery is a somber, lonely reminder of the dangers faced by those striving to summit Mount Aconcagua. It is situated at 13,000 feet (3,962 m), near the Horcones Valley, one of the main access points for Aconcagua climbers. Some grave markers reflect names and dates, while others are stacks of rocks called cairns. More than 150 climbers have lost their lives on the mountain, and several of them are buried in this cemetery. Some graves hold nothing but mementos, since bodies cannot be easily carried down from higher elevations.

than a dozen minor glaciers, known collectively as the Güssfeldt Glaciers. The glacial meltwaters descending from Aconcagua's icy slopes also feed the headwaters of the Mendoza River.

Some of the earliest inhabitants of the Aconcagua region include the Diaguitas people. From about 900 C.E., they irrigated the land and fertilized a variety of crops with fish heads and llama manure. They raised llamas and alpacas for wool. As expert metalworkers, they crafted tools, sculptures, and musical instruments. They traded with other groups as far away as Copiapó in northern Chile, a distance of more than 350 miles (563 km). Recognizing the wealth of resources surrounding Aconcagua, the Inca Empire conquered Diaguita lands in the mid-15th century.

The Inca believed that special places and objects in the natural world were gods called *huacas*. Rivers, trees, rock formations, certain animals and birds, and especially mountains were sacred beings. Pachamama was the divine Mother Earth. When the Inca looked up at the snow-capped summit of Mount Aconcagua and its neighboring peaks, they saw Pachamama. They believed Inti, the sun god, dwelt in the glaciers. His presence was said to bring the rains that melted the glaciers, triggering the annual runoff and replenishment of valley streams in spring.

The Inca built **shrines** and prayed to the *huacas*, requesting safe travels, fair weather, good harvests, and protection from injury. During prayer rituals, they made offerings of animals, fine fabric, gold, silver, and other precious objects. When they made especially important requests, such as relief from drought or the end of a spreading disease, they sacrificed their children. Human sacrifices were made to only the most powerful gods, such as Illapa, the weather god, and Inti.

The Andes Mountains have a long spiritual history with the region's people.

FIGURINE FOR AN INCAN RITUAL

For these special rituals, known as *capacochas*, children were taken to the mountains along with funeral bundles containing gifts to aid them on their journey to the afterlife. Near the mountaintops, the children were placed in shrines, where their lives were ended. The belief was that the children's spirits would act as messengers, carrying the Inca prayers directly to the gods.

In 1985, more than 450 years after the Inca Empire fell, climbers scaling Mount Pirámide, a peak attached to Mount Aconcagua, found the remnants of a *capacocha*. Sheltered within a semicircle of stacked rocks lay the mummified body of a boy. The climbers reported their find. Two weeks later, an archaeological team recovered the mummy and a funeral bundle. The mummy was immediately put in a freezer to be studied. It was found that the boy had been wearing sandals and two wool shirts that reached his knees. He had been wrapped in many layers of cotton fabric tied with cord made of plant fiber and adorned with yellow parrot feathers. The funeral bundle contained many items, including gold-covered figurines, human "dolls" with clothes and feather decorations, a rare type of oyster shell called Spondylus, finely woven cloth, and a feathered headdress. It was determined that the boy had been seven years old when a blow to the head ended his life. After decades of research, scientists and the Argentinian government decided in 2022 that the mummy and its bundle should be returned to the mountain. The remains will be placed in a protected space where hikers and climbers will be able to learn about Incan cultural history. As of early 2024, a date for the mummy's return had not been set.

The beauty and challenge of Mount Aconcagua draw climbers and hikers from around the world. But visitors take a toll. A typical summer sees more than 3,000

COST OF CLIMBING

Aconcagua climbers must buy climbing permits in the nearby city of Mendoza. Argentineans pay as little as 27,000 pesos, or about $33. Anyone from outside the country pays more. These permits vary by season, from about $1,500 in the "high season" (December 15 to January 31) and about $800 in the "middle season" (December 1–14 and February 1–20) to about $600 in the "low season" (November 15–30 and February 21 to March 15). No one is allowed to climb outside of these dates, when rescue services are not available due to the mountain's unpredictable winter storms.

mountain climbers and more than 30,000 hikers in the surrounding valleys and lower elevations. In addition, most climbers bring mules to carry their gear and supplies. All of this activity puts stress on the natural environment. People and pack animals erode the soil and trample fragile alpine plants. Gear and clothing transport seeds from other places. The resulting plants, considered invasive species, then compete with native plants for nutrients and space. Some of the mountain's plants, found nowhere else on Earth, are now threatened. Humans, their dogs, and pack animals also frighten native animals and birds away.

Perhaps the worst environmental problem is human and pack animal waste, as well as wastewater from washing, cooking, and toilets. Such waste contains nitrogen and phosphate, two substances that occur in nature and help plants grow. However, excessive amounts of these substances can have the opposite effect. Soil becomes acidified and cannot support life. Also, nitrogen and phosphate run into Aconcagua's streams, polluting the water and killing aquatic plants and wildlife. Then those contaminated streams pollute the waterways of the Mendoza River Basin, which supplies water to more than one million people and is used to irrigate crops.

All of these environmental impacts are being studied, mostly by ecologists working independently. No government plan to manage the park's ecosystem exists. And no limits are set on the number of people who can visit the park or attempt to climb Mount Aconcagua. Environmentalists are pushing for a policy that may lessen the damage being done. This could include setting a limit on annual climbing permits. For now, though, the mountain relies on its visitors to be mindful of the fragility of its unique ecosystem.

MOUNT ACONCAGUA

CHAPTER 3: HIDDEN DANGERS

Experienced climbers understand the various challenges associated with tackling the Seven Summits. But despite its height, Mount Aconcagua is a particularly popular destination for climbers with limited experience.

There are two main reasons for this. First, many mountains, such as Kilimanjaro and Everest, require climbers to travel with guides. Aconcagua has no such requirement. This means that anyone who buys a permit may attempt to climb. Second, Aconcagua is considered a "non-technical" mountain. Climbers need no special equipment, such as ropes or ice axes, on its commonly followed route. In fact, ascending the mountain along the Northwest Face, known as the Normal Route, is like hiking up a steep hill. Despite this, too many people underestimate the mountain. While the hike itself is not difficult, other factors make Aconcagua one of the most challenging of the Seven Summits. It has even been nicknamed "Mountain of Death" because of the hidden dangers that can cost climbers their lives. More

MOUNT ACONCAGUA

than 150 people have died on Aconcagua since records were kept. An average of three people perish on the mountain each year.

Two popular routes to Aconcagua's summit have been traveled and mapped—the Polish Glacier and the Normal routes. Over the decades, expert climbers have diverged from these routes, with some making treacherous and nearly impossible climbs. The most difficult path to the summit includes the roughly 9,000-foot (2,743-m) steep wall of rock and ice known as the South Face. It was first scaled by a French team in 1954. Such challenges are reserved for climbers who wish to test their skills against crumbling chunks of rock and ice, waist-deep snow, hidden crevasses, and the constant threat of an avalanche.

On the mountain's east side, the Polish Glacier is named for the Polish mountaineers who climbed the glacier to the summit in 1934. In 1960, Argentinian climbers established a shorter route, calling it the Polish Glacier Direct Route. Climbers on this route must have experience in deep snow using ropes, harnesses, ice picks, and ice tools. Most climbers—especially those with little experience—follow the Normal Route. Despite this route being easier, only about one-third of those who attempt to summit Aconcagua make it to the top. Too often people fail to plan for the mountain's hidden challenges. Common errors that inexperienced climbers make include carrying overloaded packs and then

POLISH GLACIER ROUTE

Mountain base camps offer climbers sleeping tents, food, and other basics.

falling prey to exhaustion or not taking enough supplies and running out of food and clean water.

Perhaps the worst threat to climbers comes from the altitude. Failing to properly **acclimatize** can lead to two deadly forms of altitude sickness: pulmonary edema (lung swelling) and cerebral edema (brain swelling). The air pressure at high altitudes squeezes blood vessels in the lungs and capillaries in the brain. This causes fluid to leak from the vessels and capillaries, flooding the lungs and brain. Climbers can drown in their own bodily fluid. Their brains can swell inside their skulls. Such conditions can be fatal if not treated quickly. For this reason, as soon as climbers experience symptoms—coughing, painful breathing, headache, confusion, blurred vision—Aconcagua park rangers must

BEST TOOL FOR THE CLIMB

An ice axe has a straight shaft with a sharp pick on one end and a hammer on the other. The broad pick can dig into the ground or catch on rocks, stopping climbers who fall or slide. The hammer can drive anchor pins into rock when ropes are used. An ice tool is designed for use in climbing vertical or overhanging ice. It's like an ice axe, but the shaft is bent like a hockey stick. Also, the pick is curved and very sharp. It digs deep into ice so that the tool can hold a climber's full weight.

rush to the scene to bring the afflicted climbers down the mountain. Helicopters are often used to conduct rescues.

To avoid the risks of ascending too high too fast or of getting lost, most climbers choose to hire guides or climb as part of a guided group. Guides prepare climbers with a list of supplies: cold-weather clothing, tents, **insulated** sleeping mats and bags, heaters and gas to run them, cooking pots and utensils, lamps and batteries, toilet paper and hygiene bags, food, and water. Many smaller items are necessary as well: matches, a lighter, an emergency whistle, a sewing kit and duct tape to make repairs, a Swiss army knife, sunscreen and lip balm, and sun goggles. Not everything may fit into a single backpack. Since a typical pack can weigh roughly 70 pounds (32 kg), climbers often rent mules to share the load, at least for the first part of the journey.

Some individuals have made speed-ascents up the mountain in a matter of days or even hours. However, a typical climb up and down Aconcagua takes 14 to 20 days. An adventure up the mountain begins in the city of Mendoza, Argentina, at an altitude of 2,497 feet (761 m). This is about the same elevation as Fort Worth, Texas, or Montréal, Quebec. The trip by car or bus to the Aconcagua Provincial Park takes three to four hours and ascends to 9,876 feet (3,010 m). Climbers may rent mules and head to a base camp called Confluencia at 10,827 feet (3,300 m) or a higher base camp called Plaza de Mulas (Mule Plaza), situated at 13,976 feet (4,260 m). These two permanent camps provide hot meals, showers, toilets, and Internet service. The weather might call for only a jacket and hat at this point.

MOUNT ACONCAGUA

Climbers must continue to acclimatize gradually. They typically spend three days at Plaza de Mulas. Because mules cannot climb any higher, climbers must practice carrying their own packs in the changing conditions. They do this by spending a day climbing to camps at Plaza Canadá, at 16,175 feet (4,930 m), and Nido de Cóndores (Condor's Nest), at 17,552 feet (5,350 m), before descending back to Plaza de Mulas. Resting another day helps them continue adjusting to the high altitude. Then it's back to Plaza Canadá to camp for a day and on to Nido de Cóndores to camp the day after. Here the temperatures are much colder. Climbers don insulated boots and at least three layers of clothing—including socks and gloves—topped with insulated jackets, hats, scarves, and face coverings.

Continuing upward, climbers can choose one of two camps where they will rest for a day: Berlín at 18,930 feet (5,770 m) or Plaza Cólera at 19,619 feet (5,980 m). Aconcagua's summit is just a little more than 3,000 feet (914 m) ahead, yet this final ascent can take up to 12 hours. Depending on the snow and ice accumulated during the winter, climbers may need to attach crampons to their boots and use climbing poles. Every step takes enormous determination. Breathing demands effort. Frigid wind gusts of over 100 miles (161 km) per hour may threaten to blow climbers off the mountain. At times, raging snow can make seeing where to place their next foot nearly impossible. Skin must be covered to prevent damaging sunburn and frostbite. Goggles are necessary to avoid becoming temporarily blinded by the brightness of the sun reflecting off the snow. Finally, if climbers reach the summit, they cannot linger. The danger of altitude sickness is ever present, so they will begin their descent promptly—no doubt exhilarated by their success.

MINUTES MATTER

When climbers are stricken with altitude sickness, suffer injuries from falls, or experience other medical emergencies, every minute matters. The Mendoza Police Department, park rangers, and professional climbing guides are all trained to handle rescue and evacuation during emergencies on Aconcagua. Emergency medical services are set up at the camps of Plaza Argentina on the south side and Plaza de Mulas on the north side of the mountain. Rescue teams can ascend quickly to retrieve ill or injured climbers. A helicopter service is used in extreme cases.

CHAPTER 4: RACE TO THE SUMMIT

Since ancient times, humans have felt drawn to the peaks and ranges of the world's mountains. Driven by the sheer enormity of its height, people travel from around the globe to climb the giant of the Andes—Aconcagua. Its majestic summit has long called to the human spirit of adventure and exploration.

Organized expeditions first sought the summit of Aconcagua near the turn of the 20th century, when interest stirred to measure and identify the highest points across continents. In February 1883, Paul Güssfeldt, a German mountaineer, made the initial endeavor to conquer Aconcagua's summit. He knew nothing about the mountain, but he reasoned that the north side would present the best option, since the sun would have melted much of the snow. Güssfeldt's small team, which consisted of two climbers from Chile, set up camp in the valley, then began its ascent, leaving its mules behind.

MOUNT ACONCAGUA

As the men trudged up the mountain, they quickly realized how ill-prepared they were for the mountain's fury. They had too few supplies and unsuitable gear. Halfway up, one Chilean turned back, his feet nearly frozen. Güssfeldt and his companion pressed on. They stopped to rest about 1,300 feet (396 m) below the summit. Suddenly, the mountaintop became shrouded in mist. Sleet fell from swirling, dark clouds. The pair had to retreat back down to the valley. A month later, despite an agonizing toothache that made him delirious with pain, Güssfeldt once again led his team up Aconcagua. And once again, a snowstorm drove them off the mountain before they could reach the summit.

In December 1896, a team of nine men, led by British climber Edward FitzGerald and guided by Swiss mountaineer Matthias Zurbriggen, made their first attempt to climb Aconcagua. While the team included all experienced mountain climbers, the altitude was too much for some members, and, one by one, they fell ill. Soon, only four members of the team

EDWARD FITZGERALD

SPEEDY SOLO CIRCLE

A popular climb of Aconcagua is called the 360 Route. Climbers travel around half the mountain to its summit and then down the other half—making a 360-degree circle. In 2018, adventure athlete Sunny Stroeer started from the Los Penitentes ski resort and ran up the eastern side of the mountain to the summit. Then she ran down the western side and back to the resort. The 64-mile (103-km) trek normally takes climbers 19 days, yet Stroeer completed it in just 47.5 hours. And she did it alone, setting this solo speed record for women.

MOUNT ACONCAGUA

remained, including FitzGerald and Zurbriggen. To their surprise, on December 26, the men found an odd mound of stones protecting a tin box. They opened the box and found a card with a message written in Spanish by Paul Güssfeldt. It said, "to the second entrance of the Aconcagua hill March 1883." The FitzGerald team was standing on the very spot where Güssfeldt had made the decision to turn back. As the team continued to ascend and descend, trying to acclimatize, everyone except Zurbriggen had to give up. On January 14, 1897, Zurbriggen reached the summit alone. Not everyone reading the news reports believed it was true, however. Zurbriggen had to return some years later to repeat his success and prove to the world that Aconcagua could be conquered.

In the decades after these pioneering ascents, Aconcagua increasingly became a sought-after aspiration for the boldest climbers worldwide. The remote mountain saw intensive new exploration, with routes plotted up its more demanding slopes throughout the 1930s. In 1934, a group of Polish explorers were the first to navigate the northeast face of Aconcagua, ascending a colossal glacier that extends steeply almost 2,000 feet (610 m) toward the peak. In honor of this expedition, the icy expanse was named El Glaciar de los Polacos, or the Polish Glacier. The first ascent of the 9,000-foot (2,743-m) tall South Face was by six French climbers in 1954. They struggled against

MATTHIAS ZURBRIGGEN

Snow can pile up quickly atop Mount Aconcagua, even in summer.

almost constant storms, and all but one climber lost fingers and toes to severe frostbite.

By the 1970s, about 500 people per year were attempting to summit Aconcagua, mostly along the Normal Route. Few attempted the Polish Route at that time. In 1973, a group of eight Americans decided to challenge themselves to this route. As members of an Oregon hiking and climbing club called Mazamas, the team had climbing experience. But they were not professional mountaineers. The team included a NASA engineer named John Cooper and a teacher named Janet Johnson. Like many climbers in those days, this team was ill-prepared for the mountain. They lacked the heavy sleeping bags and sturdy equipment needed for the Polish Route. After several days of fighting furious wind, deep snow, and frigid temperatures, the team had to retreat. On their way back down, Cooper and Johnson perished.

Fast forward almost 50 years: In 2020, climbers found a camera with a name stamped on it: Janet Johnson. Preserved by the cold, dry air, the film was developed, and like ghosts of the past, a series of amazing photos appeared. They showed a desolate landscape where climbers would find themselves completely cut off from the rest of the world—a world that was very different from the 21st century.

Today, Aconcagua is bustling. Permanent tents dot the landscape, providing shelter and services for the thousands of people who line up to climb. Both the Normal and Polish routes are like busy highways, with people constantly traveling up and down the mountain day after day all summer. As gear, safety equipment, and weather technology have continued to advance, the pace of

MOUNT ACONCAGUA

FRANCOIS BON

ascents has also increased dramatically, from several months to a couple weeks. Speed climbers, known as skyrunners, can reach the summit in hours.

Skyrunning is an extreme sport that involves running and hiking at high altitudes through mountainous terrain. It was officially founded in 1992 by Italian mountaineer Marino Giacometti. There are now 200 official skyrunning races worldwide, with around 50,000 participants, from 65 countries. The Skyrunner World Series, introduced in 2004, features 13 races, in 11 countries, spanning 3 continents. The first official skyrunning record at Aconcagua was set by Czech climber and runner Martin Zhor. He ran from Plaza de Mulas along the Normal Route to the summit in just 3 hours and 38 minutes. He shared on Instagram that the run was so exhausting that he crawled on all fours over the last 164 feet (50 m). He rested for 20 minutes at the summit before heading back down. In 2022, American marathon runner Tyler Andrews adopted a method of skyracing known as "light and fast." He wore only a light jacket and baseball cap from Plaza de Mulas to the summit, beating Zhor's time by six minutes.

Whether for adventure, athletic achievement, or personal enlightenment, chasing mountain summits offers humans an experience like none other. Getting to the top of a mountain such as Aconcagua is the ultimate test of one's physical and mental boundaries. This inexplicable drive to push to the limit is what has made mountain climbing an enduring human phenomenon.

FLYING OFF THE MOUNTAIN

In 2008, Frenchman Francois Bon made the first speed-riding descent of Aconcagua. Speed riding is a blend of skiing and high-speed paragliding. Bon climbed the Normal Route, carrying only a Gin NANO mini glider, helmet-camera, first-aid kit, and skis. He summited in roughly 11 hours. Then he attached his skis and slipped into the glider harness. Under the glider's 17-foot (5.2-m) wingspan, Bon leaped off the mountaintop. Reaching speeds of over 90 miles (145 km) per hour, he descended the South Face of Aconcagua in only 4 minutes and 50 seconds.

CHAPTER 4: RACE TO THE SUMMIT

MOUNT ACONCAGUA

STORIES OF THE SUMMIT

TYLER ARMSTRONG

After six months of training that included jogging on a treadmill while wearing a weighted backpack, nine-year-old Tyler Armstrong broke a world record as the youngest person to summit Mount Aconcagua. Tyler and his dad reached the top on December 24, 2013, with Tibetan mountaineer Lhawang Dhondup, an experienced Mount Everest guide. Tyler started climbing mountains with his father at age six. At age seven, Tyler set a record for summiting California's Mount Whitney in a single day. This mountain stands 14,495 feet (4,418 m) tall. When he was eight, he became the second-youngest person to scale Mount Kilimanjaro's 19,341-foot (5,895-m) peak.

When Tyler was climbing Mount Whitney, he met a boy with Duchenne muscular dystrophy (DMD). This fatal disorder causes muscles to break down. DMD mostly affects boys and often leads to death by the teen years. Moved by this encounter, Tyler made it his goal to increase awareness and fundraise for DMD research. He partnered with the CureDuchenne Foundation and has climbed for DMD ever since.

Tyler also continues to climb with Lhawang Dhondup. All told, Tyler has summited nearly 20 mountains around the world—most with Lhawang by his side. Tyler wrote in a recent Facebook post, "Without Lhawang, I wouldn't have the world record that I hold to my name today. Without Lhawang, I wouldn't know the things I know about climbing and about life."

TYLER ANDREWS

Tyler Andrews wasn't always one of the world's fastest skyrunners. He started out running cross-country in high school. Though he enjoyed it, he wasn't very fast. He had a rough start on the cross-country team at Tufts University, as well. But then he reconnected with his high school running coach, Jon Waldron, and everything changed. Tyler credits Waldron with inspiring him to focus on challenging himself instead of worrying about the competition: "Just get faster than last week," Waldron told him. By the end of his college career, Tyler had become a seven-time All-Conference runner.

Waldron's words stuck with Tyler—and so did Waldron, who continued to coach Tyler for national and international competitions. After college, Tyler moved to Quito, Ecuador, to chase his dream of running longer distances at higher altitudes. Today, he's a world-class endurance runner and trains other runners for global competitions. He's also a master skyrunner. In fact, Tyler has set or broken more than 50 records for the fastest known time running up and down mountains all around the world. His Aconcagua records include the fastest known times from the Valle de los Horcones trailhead to the summit (7 hours, 21 minutes) and from the trailhead to the summit and back (11 hours, 24 minutes). Tyler followed the route of two skyrunners who held records before him: Kílian Jornet of Spain and Swiss-Ecuadorian Karl Egloff. These are two of the most respected mountain athletes in the world, and now Tyler proudly stands—and skyruns—in the company of these masters.

MOUNT ACONCAGUA

GLOSSARY

acclimatize—to adjust or get used to a new environment

acidified—chemically changed into acid, a substance that can dissolve or burn other substances that come in contact with it

Araucanian—of an original people of central Chile and northern Argentina, living especially in the Araucania region

archaeological—relating to the study of human history by examining ancient peoples and their artifacts

contaminated—negatively affected by exposure to a polluting substance

crampon—a metal plate with spikes attached to a boot for walking or climbing on rock or ice

crevasse—a deep crack in a glacier or other body of ice

culture—a particular group in a society that shares behaviors and characteristics that are accepted as normal by that group

ecologist—a person who studies the relationships of organisms living together in an environment

evaporate—to change from liquid to invisible vapor or gas

global positioning system—a system of satellites, computers, and other electronic devices that work together to determine the location of objects or living things that carry a trackable device; GPS

insulated—protected from the loss of heat

invasive species—an organism that is not native to a particular area

lichen—an organism made up of fungus and algae growing in partnership

mummified—preserved from decay by being filled and covered with plants, minerals, and oils

navigate—to plan and follow a course of travel

sediment—material such as soil and minerals that has been broken down and deposited by wind, water, or ice

Seven Summits—a group that includes the tallest mountain on each of the seven continents

shrine—a place associated with a holy person or thing

tectonic plate—a huge, rocky piece of Earth's shell that slowly moves around the world, carrying the continents and the ocean floor with it

SELECTED BIBLIOGRAPHY

FitzGerald, Edward, et al. *The Highest Andes: A Record of the First Ascent of Aconcagua and Tupungato in Argentina, and the Exploration of the Surrounding Valleys.* London: Methuen, 1899. https://archive.org/details/cu31924021138940.

Hamill, Mike. *Climbing the Seven Summits: A Comprehensive Guide to the Continents' Highest Peaks.* Seattle, Wash.: Mountaineers Books, 2012.

Linxweiler, Eric, and Mike Maude, eds. *Mountaineering: The Freedom of the Hills.* Seattle, Wash.: Mountaineers Books, 2017.

Logan, Joy. *Aconcagua: The Invention of Mountaineering on America's Highest Peak.* Tucson: University of Arizona Press, 2011.

Ryan, Jim. *Trekking Aconcagua and the Southern Andes.* Kendal, UK: Cicerone Press, 2018.

Zimmerman, Kim Ann. "Aconcagua: Highest Mountain in South America." *Live Science,* December 8, 2017. https://www.livescience.com/41702-aconcagua.html.

WEBSITES

Aconcagua Treks
https://www.aconcaguatreks.co.uk/mountain-history.html
Review the peak's exploration history, including early photos.

Britannica
https://www.britannica.com/place/Mount-Aconcagua
Discover facts about Argentina's grand peak.

Mountain Madness
https://mountainmadness.com/blog/guest-blog-a-climber-s-journal-of-aconcagua
Read a climber's firsthand account of summiting Aconcagua.

MOUNT ACONCAGUA

INDEX

Aconcagua, Mount
    formation, 11, 12
    height, 1, 11, 12, 14
    location, 1, 11
    name origins, 20
    nickname, 28
    pronunciation, 8
    visitor numbers, 25, 27, 41
    youngest to summit, 44
Aconcagua Provincial Park, 20, 33
altitude sickness, 31, 35
Andes Mountains, 8, 10, 11, 12, 13, 20, 24, 37
Andinistas Cemetery, 22
Andrews, Tyler, 42, 45
Argentina, 1, 11, 20, 33
Armstrong, Tyler, 44
Bon, Francois, 42, 43
climate zones, 17, 19
climbing
    deaths, 22, 30, 41
    emergencies, 35
    equipment, 28, 30, 32, 41
    gear, 27, 30, 32, 38, 41
    permits, 26, 27, 28
    supplies, 27, 31, 33, 38
Cooper, John, 41
Cresta del Guanaco (Guanaco Crest), 16
Denali (McKinley), Mount, 1
Dhondup, Lhawang, 44
Diaguitas people, 23
Elbrus, Mount, 1
environmental impact, visitors', 27
Everest, Mount, 1, 11, 28, 44
FitzGerald, Edward, 38, 40
glaciers, 17, 20, 22, 23, 30, 40
    Horcones, 20, 22
    Polish, 20, 30, 40

Güssfeldt, Paul, 37, 38, 40
human sacrifices, 23, 25
Inca people, 20, 23, 25
Johnson, Janet, 41
Kilimanjaro, Mount, 1, 28, 44
Kosciuszko, Mount, 1
penitentes, 17
Plaza Canadá, 34
Plaza de Mulas, 33, 34, 35, 42
routes
    360, 39
    Normal, 30, 41, 42, 43
    Polish, 30, 41
Seven Summits, 1, 8, 28
shrines, 23, 25
skyrunning, 42, 45
snow line, 13, 17
South Face, 8, 17, 30, 40, 43
speed riding, 43
Stroeer, Sunny, 39
tectonic plates, 11, 12
temperatures, 17, 19
Valle de las Vacas (Valley of Cows), 19
Valle de los Horcones (Valley of Forks), 19
vegetation, 13, 17, 19, 20, 27
Vinson, Mount, 1
volcanoes, 12
wildlife, 13, 16, 18, 19, 20, 27
Zhor, Martin, 42
Zurbriggen, Matthias, 38, 40